Ancient Greek War and Weapons

Haydn Middleton

Heinemann
LIBRARY

www.heinemann.co.uk/library
Visit our website to find out more information about **Heinemann Library** books.

To order:
☎ Phone 44 (0) 1865 888066
🖹 Send a fax to 44 (0) 1865 314091
💻 Visit the Heinemann Bookshop at www.heinemann.co.uk/library to browse our catalogue and order online.

First published in Great Britain by Heinemann Library, Halley Court, Jordan Hill, Oxford OX2 8EJ, a division of Reed Educational and Professional Publishing Ltd. Heinemann is a registered trademark of Reed Educational & Professional Publishing Ltd.

OXFORD MELBOURNE AUCKLAND JOHANNESBURG BLANTYRE
GABORONE IBADAN PORTSMOUTH NH (USA) CHICAGO

Designed by Tinstar Design (www.tinstar.co.uk)
Illustrations by Jeff Edwards and Art Construction.
Originated by Ambassador Litho Ltd.
Printed by Wing King Tong in Hong Kong.

ISBN 0 431 145407
06 05 04 03 02
10 9 8 7 6 5 4 3 2 1

British Library Cataloguing in Publication Data
Middleton, Haydn
    Ancient Greek war and weapons. – (People in the past)
    1. Military art and science – Greece – History – To 1500 – Juvenile literature
    2. Weapons, Ancient – Greece – Juvenile literature
    3. Greece – Civilization – To 146 B.C. – Juvenile literature
    I. Title
    355'.02'0938

Acknowledgements
The Publishers would like to thank the following for permission to reproduce photographs: Acropolis Museum p7, AKG London pp6 (Erich Lessing), 14 (British Museum), 18, 23 (Erich Lessing), 38 (Erich Lessing), Ancient Art & Architecture Collection pp8, 12, 20, 22, 24, 26, 30, 32, 34, 36, 41, Ashmolean Museum p24, CM Dixon pp10, 16, 21, 30, 40, Werner Forman Archive pp37, 42 (N J Saunders).

Cover photograph reproduced with permission of Photo Archive.

Every effort has been made to contact copyright holders of any material reproduced in this book. Any omissions will be rectified in subsequent printings if notice is given to the Publisher.

The Publishers would like to thank Dr Michael Vickers of the Ashmolean Museum, Oxford, for his assistance in the preparation of this book.

Words appearing in the text in bold, **like this**, are explained in the Glossary.

Contents

The ancient-Greek world

When people talk about ancient Greece, they do not just mean the modern-day country of Greece as it used to be. The ancient-Greek world was made up of the hot, rocky mainland of Greece, plus hundreds of islands in the Aegean, Ionian and Adriatic Seas, with further overseas settlements in places ranging from northern Africa to what we now call Turkey and Italy. The earliest Greek-speakers did not think they all belonged to a single country. For a long while they did not even think they all belonged to the same **civilization**.

The ancient Greeks built one of the most creative civilizations ever seen. It was also one of the most warlike. Power was held by a number of city-states. The Greek word for a city-state was ***polis***. Each *polis* controlled the villages and farmland around it. These fiercely independent city-states or ***poleis*** had their own laws and customs, yet were seldom able to live in peace together. In the words of modern historian Oliver Taplin, 'the history of Greece is largely a history of war' – even if some of these wars did not last for very long.

The Greeks did not just fight among themselves. They invaded lands in Europe, Asia and Africa in their quest for trade, precious metals and slaves. Sometimes they even managed to fight on the same side, to defend their common Greek homeland against foreign invaders like the **Persians**. From this experience they formed a low opinion of the military skills of foreigners – all of whom they called **barbarians**. Only Greek men, they believed, knew how to fight with true courage and discipline.

From Minoans to Macedonians

For centuries the mightiest people in the Greek world were the Minoans, based on the island of Crete. Power then passed to the warlike Mycenaeans, based on the mainland region known as the **Peloponnese**. This was followed around the year 1100 BC by centuries of confusion and upheaval, but since the art of writing was also lost, we know very little about it. In the later 'Classical Age', from about 500 BC until about 300 BC, prosperity was restored

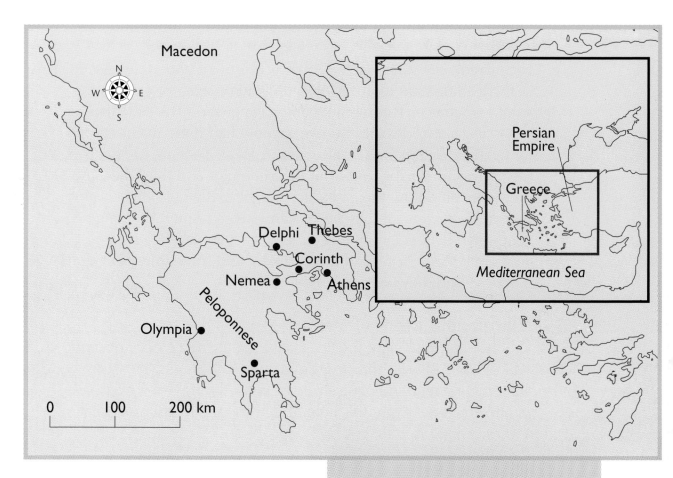

by the rise of many city-states including Athens, Sparta and Thebes. Most of the information in this book is about life in city-states like these during this period of Greek history.

Ancient Greece was not a single unified country but a collection of many separate states that often waged war on one another. The ancient Greeks used the word *Hellas* to mean all the places where there was a Greek way of life.

The city-states all had their own ways of life, and sometimes their own ways of fighting too. They were, however, united by the Greek language and by their belief that their ways were superior to those of any outside barbarians. Whether or not that was true, today – more than two thousand years since the Greek world was finally united under King Alexander the Great of Macedon, before becoming a part of the Roman Empire in 146 BC – ancient-Greek words, ideas, art-forms and attitudes still have a deep effect on us all.

War in the Greek world

Each Greek city-state wanted to be powerful. It aimed to be seen as the leading state in its region – on land or sea – or even in the whole of Greece. This often meant waging wars. The Athenian historian Thucydides said his own people had three main reasons for fighting. First, to win honour and respect. Second, to enrich themselves by seizing **loot** from their enemies and third, because they were afraid. All the city-states fought partly out of fear. They dreaded being invaded by **barbarian** foreign armies, or being conquered by a neighbouring Greek city-state. So they stayed constantly ready to defend themselves – and sometimes struck first if they sensed they were in danger.

'The glorious deeds of men'

Thucydides wrote eight thrilling books about the **Peloponnesian** War of 431–404 BC. This struggle for supremacy between Athens and Sparta ended in Sparta's victory, with Athens losing over half its **citizens**. Just before this time, the historian Herodotus wrote

Warfare in ancient times could be bloody and brutal. Once battle was joined, large numbers of lives could be lost as the army of one state aimed to prove its superiority over another.

a brilliant account of the earlier wars between the Greeks and **Persians**. He was the first man to call his work 'history' (the Greek word *historia* meant 'enquiries'). Whereas some Greek artists and writers were keen to glorify warfare, Thucydides looked deeper and found problems. He showed how, under the stress of conflict, people behaved in different and often unacceptable ways. 'Even the meanings of words,' he wrote, 'are changed. Reckless daring is believed to be loyal courage … Frantic energy is believed to be a true quality in a man. The lover of violence is always trusted and his opponent suspected.'

'Kudos' and loss

Countless Greek vases show a soldier preparing to go out to war. Maybe his wife is shown polishing up his shield – blackened from hanging in the chimney corner during the period of peace beforehand. (That period may have been quite short. Between 500 and 300 BC, Athens was at war for two years out of every three.) Warfare was seen as a noble, manly pursuit. The fame and glory won in wartime was called 'kudos'. We still use the word today, to mean the credit you earn for doing something good. Warfare was also tragic in ancient times. When many young warriors died in Samos, the Athenian statesman Pericles declared, 'It was as if the spring had been taken from the year,' by which he meant they had all been cut down in their prime.

The greatest war of all

In ancient times, the city of Troy stood on the west coast of what is now Turkey. Around a century ago, its ruins were discovered and **excavated** by archaeologists. Some historians believe that it was destroyed by a Greek fleet and army in about 1210 BC. The ancient Greeks had many legends about this 'Trojan War'. Around 800 to 700 BC, the poet Homer recorded some of them in his marvellous long poem, the *Iliad*. We know very little about Homer. He may not even have written the poem himself, but passed it on **orally** to others.

This painting shows the legendary Greek hero Achilles in one of his battle-frenzies. In the *Iliad*, Homer described how he 'stormed all over the field like some inhuman being, drawing men on and killing them. And the black earth ran with blood.'

A source and an influence

The *Iliad* describes the fighting at Troy. For nine years, according to legend, the Greeks **besieged** the city without success. Then in the tenth year it fell because of a trick. The Greeks pretended to give up, and left behind a huge wooden horse. Thinking it was a religious offering, the Trojans dragged it inside their walls. Greek warriors were hidden in the horse and they sprang out and ransacked the city. This event may never have actually happened. Throughout Homer's poem however, there are many details about ancient-Greek weapons and armour that are useful to historians.

The *Iliad* had a huge effect on later writers and artists. In the *Aeneid* by the Roman poet Virgil, a survivor of the Trojan War rebuilt Troy at Rome. A British legend then told how this survivor's great-grandson travelled west to build the city of New Troy – later called London. Ancient-Greek soldiers too were heavily influenced by the Trojan legends, which they knew as well as we know stories about the First and Second World Wars. Their own dreams were the same as those of the warriors at Troy: to win eternal fame for great military deeds.

Alexander and Achilles

Among the many ancient people influenced by the legendary Trojan War was Alexander the Great. He conquered a vast empire that stretched deep into Asia from his native Greek-speaking kingdom of Macedon. His own hero was the mighty warrior Achilles, the most effective killer in Homer's poem. In 334 BC, Alexander paid homage at a tomb that was supposed to mark the Greek warrior's resting place. He is also said to have carried a copy of the *Iliad* with him in the King of **Persia's** casket, as he fought his way as far east as the Indus River in modern Pakistan. Like his hero, however, Alexander died young.

Who were the Greek warriors?

The Greeks loved to tell each other war stories featuring **aristocrats**, kings and princes. Often these heroes were pitted against each other in single combat, and sometimes a single feat could turn the tide of a whole battle.

Real-life warfare in ancient Greece was a different matter. Many Greek soldiers were just citizens who took up arms when war broke out. You can find out a lot about them on the following pages. They fought not as individuals but shoulder-to-shoulder with their fellow-**citizens**, showing great bravery and discipline in defending their communities.

War-torn Greece

Herodotus, who is sometimes called the first-ever historian, recorded a sad proverb: 'In peace, sons bury their fathers; in war, fathers bury their sons.' War, in other words, can change the normal way of things. The Greeks liked to think of peacetime as more normal than wartime but they still spent a lot of time fighting.

This vase from Athens, dating from around 490 BC, is one of many from ancient Greece that show preparations for battle. The central soldier is arming himself.

Reminders of war were everywhere too – in theatre performances, in the tombs of the dead, in victory monuments and in the sculptures that stood in temples. In some private houses, arms and armour were hung up on the walls, while bowls and cups were decorated with scenes of battles.

Why did the Greeks fight so much? According to Thucydides, the Athenian historian, 'We believe that it is divine, and know for certain that it is universally human … to rule whatever one can.' The city-states fought against invading **barbarians** for the right to rule over themselves, and among one another to win leadership over all, or part, of Greece. This gave Greek warriors many chances to win glory on the battlefield. Some of them became very famous. After a great victory over the **Persians** in 490 BC, 'the men who fought at Marathon' were remembered as an inspiration by generations of Athenians. At the Battle of Thermopylae, in 480 BC, a thousand Spartans won lasting fame for defending a mountain pass in central Greece against a far greater Persian force.

A soldier's life

Greek writings from ancient times tell us how people felt about fighting. Part-time soldiers fought bravely for their city-states, but had families back at home to worry about. These families expected them to return in glory. Less heroic warriors, accepting that a battle was lost, sometimes threw down their shields and ran. The poet Archilochus regretted the loss of a perfect shield which he left behind on the battlefield: 'Some enemy now has the use of it, but I have saved my life. What care I for that shield? One day I'll buy another, just as good.'

Greek versus Persian

The **Persian** Empire grew vast under Cyrus the Great, who lived from 585 to 529 BC, absorbing the eastern half of the Greek world. Darius I then conquered the Greek states of Thrace, Scythia and Macedon, and was determined to conquer the southern regions of Greece too. Then the Greeks of Ionia rose in revolt against him. In 498 BC the Athenians sent some warships to assist them. They could not help the Ionians to secure their freedom. The Greeks did manage to burn Sardis, the Persian capital city of Lydia. Darius vowed to take revenge. He ordered his ***majordomo*** to tell him three times a day to 'remember the Athenians.' That is why Herodotus later wrote that the Athenian ships of 498 BC 'were the beginning of evils for both Greeks and **barbarians**.'

The Greeks pool their resources

In 490 BC, Darius sent a huge army, said to be 100,000 strong, to attack the Greek coast. The Athenians opposed them on the plain of Marathon with ten times fewer men, yet somehow they managed to overcome them. **Casualty** figures in ancient times were often exaggerated by historians on the side of the victors, but 6400 Persians were said to have been killed, with only 192 Greeks losing their lives.

This wine vase from the 4th century BC shows Greek and Persian soldiers engaged in single combat. Greek artists often showed noble Greek warriors fighting naked, while their barbarian enemies were shown clothed and wearing protective armour.

Darius died before he could attack Greece again. His son Xerxes took up the cause, and invaded in 480 BC with an army, according to one Greek writer, of five million men! (By contrast, only about 250,000 people lived in the whole densely-populated region of Attica, where Athens was.) A number of city-states joined forces to oppose them, but were powerless to prevent a Persian victory at Thermopylae. The Persians then burned Athens to the ground, but were defeated in a sea-battle at Salamis, and finally at the land-battle of Plataea in 479 BC.

By pulling together, the Greeks had fended off the Persian threat. They felt they were helped by their superior political system. For they were free men, unlike the Persians who had to obey an **autocratic** ruler. As an exiled Spartan told Xerxes, the Greeks obeyed only their own laws, not any human master.

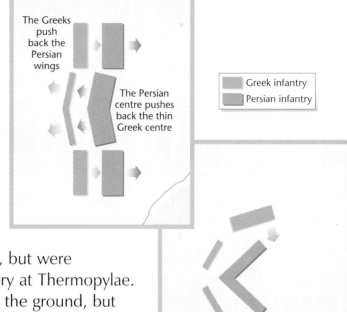

The Greeks push back the Persian wings

The Persian centre pushes back the thin Greek centre

Greek infantry

Persian infantry

The Greek wings attack the centre

At the battle of Marathon in 490 BC, the heavily outnumbered Greeks won by attacking on the wings and trapping many Persians who had broken through at the centre.

Hubris

Many Greeks believed in the idea of *hubris*. This meant that rich rulers would always strive to become greater, but then the gods would become envious and inevitably strike them down. Herodotus wrote that at the Battle of Salamis 'it was the Athenians who, *after the god*, repulsed the Persian king.' By this he meant that the Greek soldiers succeeded only because the gods had already decided that the mighty Persians should not have victory. 'Do you see,' asked Herodotus, 'how it is always the greatest houses and the tallest trees that the god hurls his thunderbolts at?'

Greek versus Greek

After the **Persian** invasions, more than 200 Greek city-states and islands joined together in a new anti-Persian alliance – to raid the **barbarians'** own lands. Since its headquarters were on the island of Delos, it was called the Delian League. Gradually it turned into an empire, with mighty Athens at its head. The Athenians protected the other city-states and in return made them pay a kind of tax called 'tribute' to finance this protection. In 454 BC the League's treasury was moved from Delos to Athens.

In the absence of a serious threat of attack from abroad, some of the city-states began to resent the power that Athens had over them. Sparta, in the southern region known as the **Peloponnese**, was particularly opposed. Finally, Sparta joined with other like-minded city-states to put an end to the wealth and power of Athens. After forming the Peloponnesian League, they declared war on Athens in 431 BC.

This bust shows the Athenian statesman Pericles, wearing his general's helmet. He presided over the Golden Age of Athens, when – under his direction – some of the city's greatest buildings were constructed.

The twenty-seven year nightmare

At first there was a **stalemate** in the war. Athens could not be defeated at sea; Sparta could not be defeated on land. The Athenians seemed safe behind their great defences, but an outbreak of plague in 430–429 BC struck down many of their leading men, including Pericles. Under his successor, Cleon, there were terrible brutalities. When Melos revolted against Athens, the Athenians killed its men and enslaved its women and children. When the Spartans captured Plataea, they too carried out mass slaughter.

Finally, in 415 BC and 405 BC, the Athenians suffered two disastrous naval defeats. Helped by Persian money, in 404 BC the Spartans captured Athens and then took over their empire. Maybe they suffered from *hubris* too. In 371 BC and 362 BC the Spartans in turn were overcome by the armies of Thebes. The balance of power was constantly shifting in the Greece of the quarrelsome city-states.

Powerful Pericles

From 463–429 BC the most important man in Athens was Pericles. He came to power after the defeat of the Persians, and played a major part in developing Athenian **democracy**. He was a great **orator**, but many comic plays of the time made fun of him. He died in the plague that hit Athens soon after the Peloponnesian War broke out. 'He was able to control the multitude in a free spirit,' wrote Thucydides. 'He led them rather than was led by them.' His war strategy for Athens was to avoid land battles and make seaborne attacks on the Peloponnese, so that the strength of the Spartans would gradually be reduced.

Magnificent Macedonians

While the city-states quarrelled among themselves, a mighty new power arose on the wild northern borders of Greece: Macedon. Its people did not all speak Greek and they were ruled over by kings. From 359 BC their monarch was Philip II, who proved to be one of history's great generals. He trained a large full-time army to fight for him with utter devotion. His **infantrymen** were armed with a thrusting **pike** or *sarissa* that could be more than 5 metres long. They formed 'Macedonian **phalanxes**' – densely-packed squares of warriors carrying shields for protection and bristling with spears – which linked up to awesome effect with swift-moving, highly-disciplined **cavalrymen**.

Philip's first aim was to unite all the Greek city-states under Macedon. In this he succeeded, finally crushing a city-state alliance at Chaeronea in 338 BC. His next aim was to invade Persia. This was in revenge, he claimed, for the **Persian** invasion of Greece 150 years before. In 336 BC, however, he was stabbed to death by a young bodyguard called Pausanias. 'Nothing has changed,' said the son who succeeded him, 'except the name of the king.' The new king's name was Alexander, and in his reign of just under thirteen years he would achieve more than even Philip could have dreamed of.

Made some time between 359 and 336 BC, this Greek coin features Philip II racing a chariot. It celebrates the king's great success in the Olympic Games of 356 BC. As a military and sporting hero, he was a great inspiration to his people.

An empire in three continents

The map below shows Alexander the Great's triumphant trail of conquest. Setting out with an army of 30,000 foot soldiers and 5000 cavalrymen, he not only defeated the Persians in 334 BC at the Granicus River, he then marched on to overcome Tyre, Egypt and the eastern part of the Persian Empire. Then on again into India where he seized the Kingdom of Poros in 326 BC. Even *his* ultra-loyal troops were too weary to expand his empire any further after that. Paying his soldiers from the **loot** he seized as he went, Alexander founded cities all along his route, where **Hellenistic** or Greek-style civilization then took root. He died in Babylon (see map) in 323 BC at the age of 32, already a figure of legend.

God-like conqueror

Alexander was a brilliant general. He led his armies over vast distances at great speed, but always kept up their **morale** – and he was a master at devising the right tactics for each battle they fought in. He saw himself as almost mythical – encouraging the people of his enormous empire to worship and adore him like a god. The earliest surviving accounts of his life date from Roman times, several centuries after he died. So we cannot be sure how Alexander intended to run his empire. We do know he was not narrow-minded – giving top jobs to Persians as well as Greeks, and adopting some Persian customs.

This map shows the enormous empire conquered by Alexander the Great.

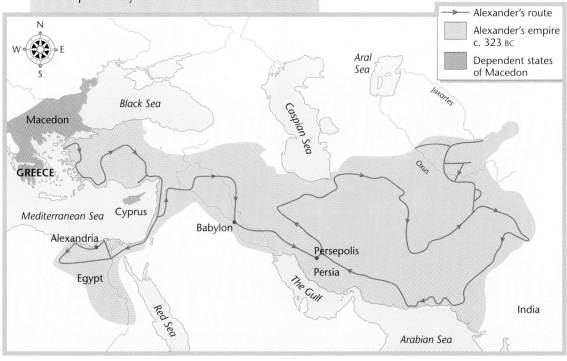

The citizen-soldier

In ancient Greece, wars were not large-scale but they could still be brutal. As the 5th century BC began, the armies of the city-states were quite small. Battles were dominated by foot soldiers called 'hoplites'. These were fully armoured spearmen, whose main defence was a round wooden shield strengthened with bronze. In fact, they took their name from the Greek word for a shield. The masters of hoplite warfare were the Spartans. Partly this was due to the strict way that future Spartan soldiers were brought up and trained. Elsewhere in Greece, hoplites were very much part-time, unprofessional soldiers.

These young hoplites are preparing themselves for battle. The warrior in the foreground is putting on one of his greaves, to protect his shin. Some hoplites also wore padding beneath their greaves.

Who could be a hoplite?

Not every able-bodied man in a city-state fought as a hoplite. That honour was reserved for **citizens** from the upper and middle classes. Sometimes these men were called 'those who provide their own shields' – that is, they had to be sufficiently well off to supply their own arms and armour.

As the Spartan poet Tyrtaeus put it, everyone admired 'the young man who remains steadfast unceasingly in the front ranks.' So there was little difficulty in enforcing the law that all adult male citizens had to serve as hoplites in times of war. In 5th-century BC Athens, this was about a third of the population. Except in Sparta, it was usually left up to the individual how much he trained. Some élite units, like the 300 strong Theban Sacred Band, did train together. In Athens, *ephebes* aged eighteen to twenty gained military experience by patrolling the countryside and, by the 330s BC, they were trained for a full year in hoplite fighting too.

Soldier behind a shield

The hoplite shield was round, 3 feet (1 metre) wide and weighed about 7 kilograms. The carrier wore it on his left, passing his arm through a ring to a grip held in the left hand. It covered most of the carrier's body, and left his right arm free to wield a thrusting spear that was 7 or 8 feet long. This spear was his main weapon, even though he carried a short sword too. On his head he wore a metal helmet, with body-armour called a **corselet** around his torso and shin-guards called **greaves** on his legs. Although there were no modern-style 'uniforms' in the early 5th century BC, hoplites in the same army might carry a common 'field sign'. For instance, a helmet or shield painted in some distinguishing colour. This would show them in the heat of battle who was on their side.

Fighting in formation

To stand any chance of success in battle, hoplites had to be brave and skilful. They also needed to be extremely well disciplined. For although their individual skills were vital, they were also part of a much larger team. The team that the hoplites fought in was called a **phalanx**.

All for one and one for all

Phalanxes were densely-packed squares of warriors that advanced against each other at a running trot. A hoplite's shield would cover his left side, while his neighbour's shield gave him some protection on the right. Each phalanx was like an enormous hedgehog, bristling with spears. These were thrust forward in an orderly, over-arm fashion. The moment of impact must have been awesome, as spear clashed with spear, and shield with shield.

According to the historian Thucydides, every hoplite 'brings his unprotected side as near as possible to the shield of the man drawn up on his right and believes that density of formation is the best protection.' Once the formation broke, it was every man for himself.

If the hoplites in the first line fell, then those in the lines behind kept on coming forward to take over, trampling the dead and wounded underfoot. Finally, when one phalanx broke and the surviving men inside it fled, the battle was over.

The Macedonian monarchs, Philip II and Alexander used their **infantrymen** in a different way. The men in a 'Macedonian phalanx' had longer spears than the Greek hoplites and smaller shields. With regular training, they learned to be flexible in battle, although their main duty was to defend rather than attack. Sometimes their job was to pin down part of an enemy line, while their cavalry launched an attack on the flank or rear. Just as in the city-states' armies, discipline was very important.

This is a lightly-armed *peltast* – named after his oddly-curved shield or *pelte*. *Peltasts* specialized in hit-and-run attacks on more heavily-armed men.

Bogeymen to the hoplites

In the mountainous north-west of Greece, the Thracians developed their own form of warfare. Sometimes city-state armies made use of their specialist warriors, called *peltasts*, in a supporting role in battles. These lightly armed men were feared by the hoplite 'as little children fear the bogeyman', according to Xenophon, an ex-soldier who wrote history books. Equipped with a long javelin and short sword, the *peltast* was protected only by a light shield of wicker or hide. This meant he could run forward, throw his javelin, then dart quickly back again. Sometimes the more heavily-armed hoplites might try to chase him, lose their formation, and so be picked off in hit-and-run attacks from other *peltasts*.

Spartan supermen

In the 5th century BC the warriors of one city-state had a reputation second to none. This was Sparta, where life was very different from elsewhere in ancient Greece. There, children became the state's property as soon as they were born. At seven, boys were sent to a **barracks**-like boarding school, where they were educated but also trained for the hardships of war. They were allowed only one cloak a year, it was said, and they slept on rushes gathered from the river.

All male **citizens** became soldiers on leaving school, and they then had to devote all their time to serving the city-state. If they married, they were not even allowed to live with their wives until they were 30. Meanwhile, the Spartans' farming was done for them by a previously conquered people called **helots**, who far outnumbered the Spartans themselves.

This statue now stands at Thermopylae as a memorial to the thousand Spartans and their king, Leonidas, who died gallantly in a battle against the **Persians** here in 480 BC.

Men or beasts?

In the words of historian Oliver Taplin, the Spartan warrior's purpose in life was 'to be one of 10,000 identical component parts in a war machine.' Many scholars and artists in other parts of ancient Greece disapproved of this single-mindedness. 'It is the standards of civilized men not of beasts that must be kept in mind,' wrote the **philosopher** and scientist Aristotle, 'for it is good men not beasts who are capable of real courage. Those like the Spartans who concentrate on the one and ignore the other in their education turn men into machines.' However, Sparta's own poet Tyrtaios expressed the Spartan ideal in this verse, when he encouraged all soldiers to be prepared to die gladly:

'Be brave, fear not the number of the enemy
Stand straight in the front of
rank with your shield before you
and see your life as your enemy; the darkness of
death should be as welcome as the light of the sun.'

The Spartans were fearsomely effective at close combat.

Spartan guts

An ancient legend told of a young Spartan boy who stole a fox and hid it under his cloak. While the creature was there, it began to gnaw at the boy's stomach. The boy did not cry out, since that would have drawn attention to him. So the fox went on eating, and in the end the boy collapsed and died of his wounds. The moral of the legend was that he died with his honour intact. If he had publicly hurled the fox away from him, he would have been disgraced – not for stealing but for having been found out. The aim of the Spartan military education system was to produce men who might show similar courage in times of war.

Mounted warriors

Xenophon's *Anabasis* was an eyewitness account of a **mercenary** expedition into the heart of Persia. When confronted by the awesome **Persian** cavalry, the Greek foot soldiers took fright. It had to be explained to them that 10,000 men on horseback were only really 10,000 men: 'For no man ever perished in battle from being bitten or kicked by a horse.' The foot soldier could in fact strike harder and with truer aim than the horseman, who had to take great care not to fall off his **steed**! For most Greeks, until the time of Alexander the Great, horses featured little in their battles.

These marble cavalrymen decorated the Parthenon Temple in Athens, which was built in the mid 5th century BC. Note how the riders sit astride their horses without either saddles or stirrups to help keep them balanced.

The drawbacks of horses

Only the rich could afford to keep horses in ancient Greece. Some wealthy warriors rode to battle, then dismounted and fought on foot. This was partly because it was thought nobler to be a foot soldier. It was also because fighting on the backs of small Greek horses was tricky. The rocky, uneven ground was hazardous for horses without horseshoes – and since the saddle and stirrups had not yet been invented, warriors struggled to sit steadily enough to use swords or *kamaxes* (long, thin spears).

In flat regions like Thessaly in northern Greece, where horse-handling was easier, **cavalrymen** played an important part in armies. In their distinctive cloaks, tunics and broad-brimmed sun-hats, Thessalians were known as the finest horsemen in Greece. By the early 4th century BC, most city-states had small cavalries. The horsemen could be used for **reconnaissance** too, and to pursue retreating enemies. Then Alexander made a great leap forward in using his skilful, swift, highly-trained 'Companion cavalrymen' to work to devastating effect alongside his 'Macedonian **phalanxes**' of hoplites. Alexander also brought back over a hundred elephants on his return from India, but he never got a chance to use them in a **pitched battle**.

Equipping an Athenian cavalryman

The cavalry of Athens was expanded to about 1000 men before the **Peloponnesian** War of 431–404 BC. Every year the Athenian council inspected both horses and men for fitness for service. Horses that did not come up to scratch were branded on the jaw with the sign of a wheel. Tomb monuments show that around this time Athenian cavalrymen wore: a sleeveless tunic like a modern vest under a bronze **cuirass**, with a wide-brimmed Thessalian-style sun-hat or sun-hat-shaped helmet on the head, and thin boots on the feet. For weaponry, he carried a *kamax*, maybe a pair of javelins too, and a cavalry **sabre**, which might have had a curved blade.

Light-armed troops

The hoplites thought that only they themselves fought in a noble, 'manly' way. Yet ancient-Greek armies often included lighter-armed troops too, who served as archers, javelin-throwers or stone-slingers. In a play by Euripides, a character compared the experiences in battle of hoplites and archers. A hoplite's life depended on the courage of his comrades, he said, and he was left defenceless if his spear broke, but an archer could fire up to 10,000 arrows at the enemy – and he stood far enough away not to be attacked himself.

An ancient-Greek archer shows here how he could go about his business even when he was on the run!

An archer could actually carry only fifteen to twenty arrows in his carrying-case or 'quiver', and the firing-distance of a Greek bow was only 80–100 metres. In addition, the arrows could probably not pierce hoplite shields. A javelin, too, could be thrown no further than twenty metres and a thrower could carry only a few of them. As for stone-slingers, or slingers of lead 'bullets', they could do damage – but without a lot of training, they were unlikely to be very accurate. All these types of warrior were useful in attacking or defending city walls and, unlike hoplite **phalanxes**, they did not need flat ground to fight on. When it came to **pitched battles**, 'hoplites ruled' throughout the Classical Age which lasted from around 500 BC until around 300 BC.

Unfree warriors

Slaves served their masters on the field of battle just as they did at home. Sometimes called 'shield-bearers' or 'baggage-carriers', they personally attended hoplites and **cavalrymen** on campaign. They did more than carry equipment, put up tents and cook food. They might also actually fight as lightly-armed troops. At the Battle of Plataea in 479 BC, Herodotus wrote that seven light-armed **helots** were stationed with each Spartan hoplite, to protect him. The Spartans even sent whole armies of freed helots to go on long-distance campaigns in northern Greece and in Asia Minor.

Mercenaries

Mercenaries were professional warriors who fought for pay, unlike **citizen**-soldiers who fought for the honour of their city-states. There were always mercenaries in the armies of the ancient-Greek world, and in the 4th century BC their numbers became very great. Since their only job was to fight, they were free to take part in long campaigns and in times of peace they could practise specialist skills like archery and javelin throwing. Xenophon, a mercenary commander himself, claimed that by setting a standard of excellence, mercenary troops improved the quality of the citizen-soldiers they fought with. However, there was always the fear that they might desert for higher pay elsewhere.

Preparing for battle

Xenophon wrote that a **citizen** must keep himself in good condition for three main reasons. Firstly, to be 'ready to serve his state at a moment's notice' as a warrior. Secondly, 'self-preservation also demands it' – if he is to survive in war or times of danger. Thirdly, 'what a disgrace it is for a man to grow old without ever seeing the beauty and the strength of which his body is capable!'

Here at the *palaestra*, young men exercise under the eye of a bearded trainer. Two young men wrestle, another binds his hands before boxing, while a fourth uses a pickaxe to soften up the ground for falling on.

Getting in shape

In most city-states, hoplites were only part-time warriors. They could therefore not be trained or organized like modern professional soldiers. In 5th-century BC Athens, citizen **ephebes** or young men aged eighteen to twenty had a basic period of military training. During this

they might also man forts or serve in patrols to protect Athens' borders. For the most part, the main form of training was exercise in the *palaestra* (an area for practising combat sports) or the *gymnasion* (a bigger sports complex). This was something that many Greek men – who shared Xenophon's views on the value of working out – were happy to do anyway. Some then took additional weapons training from experts.

In Sparta, training was carefully organized for every male citizen. Again this centred on athletics, but included **drill** with weapons and battle-formations too. The main aim was to fill Sparta's armies with fit, strong, agile warriors. To this end, Spartan boys in their state **barracks** were brought up to be tough and violent. Their food was rationed, so they were forced to use their wits to steal more. If caught, they were whipped for 'stealing unskilfully'. Packs of boys were set against each other in vicious ball games and fights. As they approached the age of twenty, the tests got more severe. During the *krypteia* or 'period of hiding' a boy had to live alone and under cover in the countryside, killing **helots** who were believed to be dangerous. No wonder these trainees seemed invincible when the time came for them to fight in actual battles.

In the gym

The ancient Greeks took their sport and exercise very seriously. The greatest athletes of the age won glory at the Olympic and other **Panhellenic** Games, and became legendary idols. No Greek state was meant to fight during the **truces** proclaimed when these Games were taking place. Ordinary citizens as well as star athletes could, and did, train at the local *gymnasion*. Those interested in combat sports could practise at the *palaestra*. In the sport of ***pankration***, you could use any means possible to put your opponent down. In Sparta, even biting and eye-gouging were allowed!

Battle stations

In ancient-Greek warfare, most fighting took place during the four or five months of summer. Most campaigns happened between the grain harvest in May and the grape harvest in September – or, at the latest, the November ploughing. Summer was also the safest time of year for sailing. Some rich and powerful states, however, tried to gain an advantage by extending this 'fighting season'. Philip of Macedon, according to Demosthenes, 'made no distinction between summer and winter' in pursuing his military objectives.

Clash of the phalanxes

Hoplites fought in close-packed **phalanxes**. These were effective only if the ground they fought on was level, so that they could keep in line. 'The Greeks seek out their smoothest piece of ground,' wrote Herodotus 'and go down and fight.' No army would let another have the advantage of fighting downhill.

Trumpeters signalled the charge. The forces began to walk towards each other, singing a battle-song called a *paian*. Gradually they picked up speed, broke into a run, and started whooping instead of singing. (Spartan hoplites were different. They did not run, but with great discipline advanced at a steady pace, then halted to make a pre-battle blood sacrifice in front of their enemies.)

Both Greek and **Persian** armies included trumpeters. Their blasts could signal the start of a battle. Music has always played an important part in rousing warriors into the mood for fighting.

Once the armies clashed, the outcome was mainly decided by how well the hoplites performed on the day. (See page 20 for how they fought.) Usually there was little to choose between the weapons of either side or of the numbers in either army. Battles could be short, but might last for most of a day, ending with desperate warriors using their hands and teeth. When trumpeters sounded the retreat, victory was marked by another singing of the *paian*. Then, at the point where the enemy first turned, a victory 'trophy' was set up, made of arms and armour attached to a wooden frame. Meanwhile, pipers would play and all the victors would give thanks to their gods.

Spartan haircare

The **biographer** Plutarch's account of the fearsome Spartans' way of going into battle gives some surprising details: 'In times of battles the officers relaxed the harshest elements of their discipline, and did not stop the men from beautifying their hair and their armour and their clothing … They took care over their hair from the time when they were youths, especially seeing to it in times of trouble so that it appeared sleek and well-combed, since … it makes the handsome better-looking and the ugly more frightening … It was an impressive and frightening sight to see them advancing in time to the flute and leaving no space in the battle-line, with no nervousness in their minds, but calmly and cheerfully moving into the dangerous battle to the sound of music.'

Underneath this Spartan warrior's helmet, his hair would have been very neat. According to the historian Herodotus, Spartans groomed themselves 'so that they might die with their heads tidy.'

Tilting the balance in battle

Xenophon believed that a military commander should 'devise a **ruse** for every occasion, since in war nothing is more profitable than deceit … Think about successes in war, and you will find that most of the greatest have been achieved by means of deceit.' He may have been stretching his point a little. Once two hoplite armies had started to slug it out there was little a general could do except fight well himself, as an example to his men.

This is a picture from the Middle Ages of the great Greek scientist and engineer Archimedes who lived from about 287 until 212 BC. He tried to help to defend Syracuse by inventing cranes to lift enemy ships and turn them upside down, and by using mirrors to focus the Sun's rays on the ships and so set them on fire.

Stealing a march on the enemy

Sometimes armies tried to capture a city by 'siege' – by camping around it and forcing the **citizens** to surrender. There was always room for some **ingenuity** here. An improved kind of scaling ladder was invented, to make it easier for attackers to climb city walls. Also, a ladder fitted with a shield allowed men who stood on it to make longer observations. Burning missiles might be thrown at a city to set fire to its defences, and the Athenians used battering rams to attack Samos in 440 BC. Meanwhile, great catapults were devised to keep enemy siege engines at bay. Records survive that show how carefully the Greeks calculated the distance that missiles could be fired.

On the field of battle, few tactical thinkers were greater than Epaminondas of Thebes. At the battle of Leuctra in 371 BC, the Thebans had to face a Spartan-led army. The Spartans usually put their best troops on the right wing. They expected to win an advantage there, then wheel inwards and 'roll up' the rest of the enemy line. Their plan was therefore to win the battle before their less skilled left and centre could get involved and lose it. Epaminondas responded by ranging his Theban hoplites in a column 50 ranks deep, not a wide formation. Then his column struck on the left, broke through the élite Spartan right-wing and won the battle before the lesser Theban troops could lose it. This might sound like a simple plan now, but it needed great skill and discipline to carry it out in the heat of battle.

Hannibal's sneaky snakes

The great general Hannibal, who lived from 247–182 BC, led Carthage in a great war against the Romans. Once he was in charge of a **Hellenistic** fleet. According to the Roman Cornelius Nepos, he sent his sailors ashore to make a collection of poisonous snakes – but they had to be alive. When the snakes were brought back, Hannibal had them sealed into fragile jars, then fired into the ships of the enemy. The men of the enemy fleet would have surely panicked to find the snakes escaping among them, and lost concentration for the battle ahead.

Fighting ships

The earliest Greek warships were used just to transport warriors, not to fight against other ships. After about 700 BC, fights at sea began and ships carried soldiers for boarding or defence. The most important Greek warship became the *trireme*. It had sails but was mainly powered by rowers and instead of just one line of them, as in earlier vessels, a *trireme* had three banks of up to fifty oarsmen. They were all crammed into a space about 37 metres (120 feet) long by 6 metres (20 feet) wide. The *trireme* was easily **manoeuvrable** and could travel at the fast speed of 7 nautical miles per hour.

A modern reconstruction of an ancient-Greek *trireme*. There were two masts, from which sails could be unfurled when there was a good strong wind.

All aboard

Athenian *triremes* were like little worlds in miniature. The captain, the *trierarch*, was a wealthy **citizen** who had volunteered or been appointed to the job. Under him served the **marines**, usually ten citizen hoplites, four archers, and the specialist ship's officers (a helmsman, a lookout, a rowing-master, a pipe player, a **purser** and a shipwright for emergency repairs). Then there were all the oarsmen. These could be low-class citizens, slaves, foreigners, or anyone willing to serve for pay. The hoplites on board may have looked down upon the more **menial** oarsmen. However, these professional rowers proved far more valuable than inexperienced citizens who took up oars in time of war.

Masters of the sea

In the early years of the **Peloponnesian** War (431–404 BC), Athens kept 100 ships on semi-permanent guard duty, and often employed up to 250 ships in total, with up to 50,000 men on board. Clearly the Athenians thought it vital to maintain a powerful presence on the seas. So did other city-states.

This was not only to carry out blockades or to engage in **pitched battles**. *Triremes* made sure that food supplies could be shipped safely from the Black Sea in merchant vessels. As the *Constitution of Athens* says, 'If a city is rich in wood for shipbuilding, where will it be able to dispose of it without the permission of the ruler of the sea? And the same is true of iron or bronze or sailcloth, which very things are what ships are made of. And those who rule the sea can say where they are to go.' For these reasons alone, the city-states competed for what was called *thalassocracy*, or mastery of the seas.

Naval warfare

One of the greatest naval battles took place at Salamis in 480 BC, during the **Persian** wars (see page 12). After defeat on land at Thermopylae, the government of Athens evacuated the city's women and children – then sent its male **citizens** to man the *triremes*. On receiving a false message that they were trying to flee, the Persian fleet tried to prevent the *triremes* from 'escaping' by blocking a narrow channel between the Greek mainland and the island of Salamis.

This was just what the Athenians wanted. The lighter Greek *triremes* were in fact waiting to attack the Persians, in a place where it would be hard for them to **manoeuvre**. In the end, the Persians lost almost all their ships in a crushing defeat. Some of the victors may soon have been among a theatre audience listening to actors celebrating the great event in a play by Aeschylus. With relish the playwright described how at the battle's end, the Greeks 'beat the Persians with splintered oars and planks from wrecked ships,' as if they were beating to death shoals of fish that had been caught in a net: 'Moans and shrieks sounded across the sea.'

This decoration shows ancient-Greek sea warfare, around 500 BC.

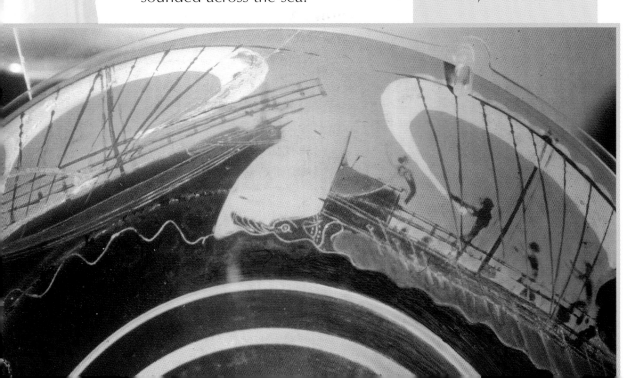

Pirates

Our word pirate comes from the Greek word for sea-robber, *peirates*. In the 4th century BC, along with shipwrecks, piracy was a growing problem for merchants in the seas around Greece. Some ancient-Greek pirates were encouraged by their governments to make raids on enemy shores and shipping. City-states made treaties with one another in an attempt to stamp out piracy, but without much success. A captured pirate once told Alexander the Great: 'Because I raid with a small boat I'm called a pirate. You do the same thing with a large army and you're called an emperor.' He had a point – for 'official' armies and navies seized as much **plunder** as they could get their hands on.

Trireme tactics

For a **pitched battle** at sea, *triremes* had to be **deployed** in a single line to face the enemy. When the two lines came close enough, the men on board might engage in what Athenian historian Thucydides called the 'old style' of combat: the *triremes* lay still, while the warriors launched missiles, or tried to enter and seize the closest enemy vessel. The 'newer' style involved manoeuvring quickly to get sideways on to an enemy *trireme*, then smashing into it with the heavy, pointed, bronze-sheathed 'ram' on the lower part of the attacking *trireme's* **prow**. A quick withdrawal was then vital, leaving the enemy in chaos – and, hopefully, throwing the whole enemy line into confusion. The eventual winners would sing a *paian* or battle-song, then build a victory 'trophy' out of arms and armour (on the nearest island), just like hoplite victors did on land.

Themistocles was the Athenian politician who masterminded the victory over the Persians at Salamis in 480 BC. He had also persuaded the Athenians to build more warships in the years leading up to the battle. This enlarged fleet, he said, would be the 'wooden walls' to keep Athens safe.

The cost of war

Warfare has always been an expensive business. In ancient Greece it cost more to wage war than to finance any other public activity – including the most massive building projects like the Acropolis in Athens. There was also, after each war, the great cost of repairing all the damage that had been done to the cities and countryside. Before the Classical Age (roughly from 500 BC to 300 BC), private individuals paid for most campaigns. Then the city-states, funded by **citizens'** taxes, took on the financial burden. In time, the winners of wars tended to be the states with the greater wealth.

Who footed the bill?

There were three main ways of paying for military campaigns. Firstly by using public funds, secondly by making the wars pay for themselves (by seizing **loot** from the enemy while the campaigning army marched along), and thirdly – and rather shamefully – by doing deals with wealthy **barbarian** states.

Sieges could take a long time and be very expensive for the besieging army. Thasos and Plataea both managed to resist their attackers for over two *years*. Many cities were captured when traitors inside betrayed the defenders.

In 483 BC, the Athenians decided to create a state-owned navy, using money from taxes. Rowers and **marines** were offered pay at a fixed daily rate. Later, hoplites and their servants were paid at the same rate, and so were **cavalrymen**. Maintaining the navy was especially expensive – so were the sieges in which paid hoplites took part. The nine-month siege of Samos cost the Athenians more than 1200 *talents* of silver. After it, in 431 BC, there were only 6000 *talents* in the whole Athenian treasury. Less wealthy states could not have coped.

The cost of a hoplite

Hoplites had to pay for their own arms and armour, their bedding and a few days' rations of bread, cheese, onions, or salted fish. When they were in friendly territory, the local people might then help them out. If they entered enemy territory, they would help themselves to whatever they needed. Therefore Greek armies did not need many supplies, or big stocks of ammunition, and often travelled with only a small baggage train or group of pack animals. All this changed if a siege had to be carried out. Then, an army needed siege machines to be brought up and plenty of supplies for the waiting warriors.

A second way of raising funds was to seize **plunder** during the fighting. Merchant ships, fishing boats or passenger ferries might be captured. On land, **booty**-sellers might sell prisoners or cattle that had been taken, and prisoners of war might be kept for ransom. This all brought money in, but there was no way of knowing in advance how much. The third source of income was more reliable. In the **Peloponnesian** War, both Athens and Sparta begged **Persian** governors and generals to **subsidize** them with gold. With backing from this former enemy of all Greece, the Spartans triumphed (see page 15).

Limiting the damage

The human cost of warfare in ancient Greece could be very high. Many wars were short and had few long-term effects, but some were devastating. The modern historian Hans van Wees calculates that during the Classical Age around twenty-four city-states were **annihilated**: 'The enemy cut the throats of the entire adult male population, made slaves of the women, children and elderly, and sold to new masters those who were slaves already … Thousands more died in each of the major battles of the age … Soldiers fell at the rate of one in seven on the losing side, one in twenty among the victors.'

What limits did the Greeks themselves put on all this devastation? For one thing, the 'fighting-season' could be confined to four or five months of each year (see page 30). For another, fighting was supposed to be suspended for religious reasons during certain 'sacred' periods. The Spartans actually refused to take part in the Battle of Marathon, since they were not allowed to start a campaign before the full moon. The superstitious Greeks also tried to predict – from observing the world around them – if it was wise or not to fight.

One warrior has already fallen in this battle. In the eyes of many Greeks, it was better to die nobly than to survive by being cowardly.

Interpreting the omens

The trouble with omens was that their meaning might be unclear. The **biographer** Plutarch described a **nocturnal eclipse** of the moon just before an Athenian night operation against the enemy: 'The men were convinced that it must be a supernatural **portent** and a warning from the gods that fearful calamities were at hand.' There was no experienced **soothsayer** in the army to give a verdict. *Was* it really an evil omen, or 'was it a positive advantage, since an operation of this kind … needs concealment above all else, while light is fatal to it'? The commander decided to take no chances, and held back his men on that night.

At the ancient Olympic Games there was a running race in full armour. A three-month-long 'Sacred **Truce**' was proclaimed when the Games took place, so that even city-states that were at war could still send athletes to take part.

After the battle

In later Classical times, when a Greek city was captured, the victors were not supposed to massacre the people inside or destroy the buildings. After a battle, it was forbidden to mutilate the bodies of the enemy dead. The victors were allowed to strip them of all their possessions, then the dead men's corpses could be taken back by their comrades. However, rules like these were not always observed. In 405 BC, at the end of the **Peloponnesian** War, around 3000 captured Athenians were executed. This was because the Athenians had earlier voted to cut off the hands of all *their* prisoners of war and, on capturing warships from Corinth and Andros, had simply thrown both crews overboard.

How do we know? – Vergina

For centuries ancient Greece was disunited. **Polis** often fought against *polis*; the many states pulled together only when there was a common threat from abroad. Then, one warlike state in the north of the Greek-speaking world grew mightier than all the rest: Macedon. Its king, Philip II, conquered the whole of Greece and brought to an end the era of the city-state. His son Alexander then expanded the new Macedonian Empire far into Asia. This was the last great achievement of ancient-Greek civilization.

Here we see what Vergina looks like today – a ghost of the military city which once served as the capital of mighty King Philip of Macedon.

Coarse, barbaric Macedonians?

In the 1970s, excavations began at Pella, the Macedonian capital after Aigai. Some of the **artefacts** discovered were the spoils of battle. Women were buried with exquisite gold jewellery, while elaborate swords accompanied the men's bodies. There were also marvellous marble sculptures, terracotta **statuettes** and bronze **figurines** of the Greek gods and goddesses. Experts used to believe that the Macedonians were a coarse, military people with little interest in finer things. These beautiful finds show they were not just the most effective and successful warriors of ancient-Greek times. When not campaigning, they and their families led luxurious, refined lives.

The tomb of King Philip

Evidence about Philip the Warrior King comes from archaeology as well as from ancient books. His capital was at a place called Aigai, later known as Vergina. In 1977, archaeologists opened up Philip's royal tomb there. In ancient times, people were often buried with their prized possessions. At Vergina the archaeologists found an ivory head that is probably meant to be an image of Philip. Other finds inside his beautifully painted tomb included a golden crown, a golden quiver for arrows, silver bowls and cups, and items of bronze armour. A pair of bronze **greaves** were also found. Since one was shorter than the other, archaeologists think they may have once belonged to Philip. This was because ancient eyewitness writers said that the king limped from a war wound. It is not surprising that so many of the prized possessions of so successful a soldier were connected with weapons and warfare.

Greece today is littered with many such ancient sites. **Excavations** by archaeologists can throw up all sorts of hidden treasures – and help historians to form a clearer picture of a time when warfare was such a regular part of life.

Timeline

All dates are BC

c.3000	Greece controlled till c.1450 by Minoan kings based on the island of Crete
c.1600–1100	Mycenaeans rule separate kingdoms in mainland Greece
c.1210	Date of possible destruction of Troy
490	Battle of Marathon
c.490–479	Main period of **Persian** invasions of Greece
480	Battle of Salamis, Battle of Thermopylae
479	Battle of Plataea
474	Syracusans defeat Etruscans at Battle of Cumae
431–404	**Peloponnesian** War between Greek city-states
371	Thebans destroy Spartan power at Battle of Leuctra
338	Philip of Macedon defeats Athens at Thebes at Battle of Chaeronea
336-323	Greece ruled by Alexander the Great of Macedon after invasion and conquest
146	Greece becomes part of Roman Empire

Sources

Alexander the Great
Robin Lane Fox
(Penguin, 1986)

Ancient Greece – Utopia and Reality
Pierre Lévêque
(Thames Hudson, 1994)

The Ancient Greek
Nicholas Vinter Sekunda
(Osprey Military, 1986)

Classical Greece
Ed. Roger Osborne
(Oxford University Press, 2000)

Europe – A History
Norman Davies
(Oxford University Press, 1996)

Greece and the Hellenistic World
Ed. John Boardman, Jasper Griffin and Oswyn Murray
(Oxford University Press, 1988)

The Greek and Macedonian Art of War
F.E. Adcock
(University of California Press, 1957)

The Greeks
Paul Cartledge
(Oxford University Press, 1993)

Political and Social Life in the Great Age of Athens
Ed. John Ferguson and Kitty Chisholm
(Ward Lock, 1978)

These Were the Greeks
H.D. Amos and A.G.P. Lang
(Hulton, 1979)

Glossary

annihilated destroyed, wiped out

aristocrats noblemen, the 'best' citizens in a state

artefacts item, useful or artistic, made by a person

autocratic way of governing by a single powerful ruler

barbarians word used by ancient Greeks to describe anyone who was not Greek

barracks buildings where soldiers live

besieged surrounded and tried to starve into surrender

biographer writer of the life-stories of others

booty items seized and kept in times of war (like loot)

casualty person who is killed or injured in warfare or an accident

cavalryman soldier who goes into battle on horseback

citizen male member of a *polis* with political rights

civilizations ways of life common to particular groups of people

corselet armour that covered the trunk of the body

cuirass breastplate and back-plate fastened together to protect a soldier's body

democracy kind of government in which people can elect their own rulers

deployed organized in battle formation

drill instruction or training in military exercises

ephebes Athenian men aged eighteen to twenty, on military service

excavated dug up

excavations digs made by archaeologists

figurines statuettes, small figures

greaves pieces of armour that protected the shins

Hellenistic in the Greek style (*Hellen* was Greek for 'a Greek')

helots conquered people who worked for the Spartans

hubris pride that will lead to punishment by the gods

infantrymen soldiers who go into battle on foot

ingenuity cleverness, quick-wittedness

loot items seized and kept in times of war (like booty)

majordomo chief official in a royal household

manoeuvrable easy to manoeuvre

manoeuvre to plan and control a movement

marine soldier trained to serve on land or sea

menial low-grade

mercenary soldier who fights purely for pay

morale confidence and enthusiasm

nocturnal eclipse passing of one heavenly body (planet or star) in front of another, at night

orally in spoken form

orator public speaker

Panhellenic relating to the whole of Greece and all its people

pankration ferocious Olympic combat sport

Peloponnese region of southern Greece, including Sparta (see map on page 5)

Persians people of an ancient Middle-Eastern kingdom, now the modern country of Iran

phalanx group of soldiers banded tightly together for battle

philosopher seeker after wisdom and often a teacher of great knowledge

pike thrusting weapon like a spear

pitched battle battle in which the time and place are arranged beforehand

plunder items seized and kept in times of war (like booty)

poleis plural of *polis,* meaning city-states

polis Greek word for city-state

portent omen

prow front of a ship

purser officer who keeps accounts on board a ship

reconnaissance checking out the 'lie of the land' and the enemy's position

ruse trick

sabre cavalryman's sword, with a curved blade

soothsayer someone who can foretell the future

stalemate deadlock, neither side winning

statuettes small statues, usually of people

steed horse, especially one used in warfare

subsidize give financial assistance, help to pay the cost of something

talent very large unit of Greek currency

truce time when fighting was temporarily stopped

Index

Titles in the *Ancient Greek* series include:

Hardback   0 431 14550 4

Hardback   0 431 14541 5

Hardback   0 431 14543 1

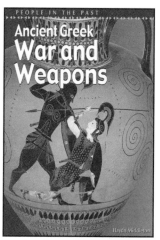

Hardback   0 431 14540 7

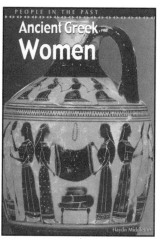

Hardback   0 431 14542 3

Find out about the other titles in this series on our website www.heinemann.co.uk/library